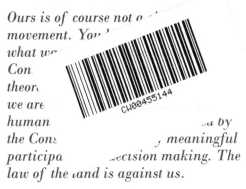

Ours is of course not a ... movement. You ... what w... Con... theor... we are human ... ...a by the Con... ... meaningful participa... ...ecision making. The law of the land is against us.

Speaking to an American audience in 1986.

Following the struggle to end apartheid, racial discrimination more generally, and have political detainees – including Nelson Mandela – released from prison in apartheid era South Africa, political organisations were finally unbanned in 1990. 1984 Nobel Peace Prize laureate Archbishop Desmond Tutu played a seminal role in all this.

Through his deeds and words Archbishop Desmond Tutu earned the disdain, but increasingly the grudging respect, of many of the leading figures upholding apartheid South Africa's brutal system of rule, stemming ultimately from the bygone colonial era.

His tireless efforts to convince his compatriots of the justice of the cause of black South Africans in a country obsessed by racial thinking were met by much effort to discredit him over the years; especially because his campaign reached far beyond the borders of South Africa. It was this latter fact that more than likely saved his life. Despite the attempts to vilify him, the justice of the cause he championed was confirmed when he introduced the freshly released Nelson Mandela to the world in 1990. Tutu was then instrumental in maintaining calm where he could during the protracted negotiated political settlement in South Africa. He was chosen to lead a special commission – the Truth and Reconciliation Commission – that pioneered a method of allowing citizens and perpetrators to reflect on and hopefully progressively come to terms with the effect of unjust political rule. His support of the cause of those oppressed by unjust principles wherever they happen to exist, using basic principles of democratic struggle, continues to shame those responsible into realising their folly.

In the Words of Desmond Tutu conveys the intelligence, dignity, steadfastness and much admired wit with which Desmond Tutu goes about his work. In doing that it explains how he came to symbolise, and indeed mould, a growing movement for global justice.

David Shepherd is a South African freelance researcher

In the Words of
Desmond Tutu

A Little Pocketbook

Compiled and edited by
David Shepherd

PENGUIN BOOKS

PENGUIN BOOKS

Published by the Penguin Group

Penguin Books (South Africa) (Pty) Ltd, 24 Sturdee Avenue, Rosebank, Johannesburg 2196, South Africa

Penguin Books Ltd, 80 Strand, London WC2R 0RL, England

Penguin Group (USA) Inc, 375 Hudson Street, New York, New York 10014, USA

Penguin Group (Canada), 90 Eglinton Avenue East, Suite 700, Toronto, Ontario, M4P 2Y3, Canada (a division of Pearson Penguin Canada Inc.)

Penguin Ireland, 25 St Stephen's Green, Dublin 2, Ireland (a division of Penguin Books Ltd)

Penguin Group (Australia), 250 Camberwell Road, Camberwell, Victoria 3124, Australia (a division of Pearson Australia Group Pty Ltd)

Penguin Books India Pvt Ltd, 11 Community Centre, Panchsheel Park, New Delhi – 110 017, India

Penguin Group (NZ), 67 Apollo Drive, Mairangi Bay, Auckland 1310, New Zealand (a division of Pearson New Zealand Ltd)

Penguin Books (South Africa) (Pty) Ltd, Registered Offices:
24 Sturdee Avenue, Rosebank, Johannesburg 2196, South Africa

www.penguinbooks.co.za

First published by Penguin Books (South Africa) (Pty) Ltd 2010

Copyright © Penguin Books, 2010
Compiled and edited by David Shepherd

ISBN 978 0 143 02684 6

Typeset by Nix Design in 10.7/13.5pt Bodoni
Cover design: mr design
Printed and bound by CTP Book Printers, Cape Town

Dedication

This book is dedicated to the many people who over the years have become aware of – and perhaps assisted – Nobel Peace Prize laureate Archbishop Emeritus Desmond Mpilo Tutu's work to advance the cause of oppressed people. His life is a testament to courage. The spirit in which he carries out that work continues to assist in breaking the chains of loyalty to transient, man-made conceptions of how one ought to live, and how societies ought to be run. Desmond Tutu exemplifies how to reach instead to older principles that can inform how stable societies are brought about and maintained, and connects them to modern life.

This collection is dedicated to South Africans in general as something to inspire us to continue to meet challenges we face, and will continue to face.

Acknowledgements

Thanks to all those who have taken so much care in researching the life and times of Archbishop Desmond Mpilo Tutu over the last 30 years. Without this work it would be difficult to differentiate between important truths and distortions, which were for many years part of organised efforts to blunt the message of the archbishop in his work to end apartheid; efforts that remain inseparable from his ministry.

John Allen's authorised biography of Desmond Tutu, *Rabble-Rouser for Peace*, was particularly helpful, as were the journalists who have followed the involvement of Archbishop Tutu in his extensive charitable work, and wide-ranging participation in efforts to broker change in various unjust political situations over the years.

Introduction

In the period leading up to the negotiated political settlement, which was still a work in progress when societal forces were extremely fragmented, state security forces were notorious for provoking internecine violence among the population.

Anglican Archbishop Tutu and other bishops were in Sebokeng township celebrating Eucharist and visiting those injured in just such an example of recent violence. A crowd of 3 000 young people were gathered in a volatile area of the township known as Beirut. Tutu got out of his car to speak to some of the assembled, many of whose companions had been shot by the police or troops two days earlier. Journalist John Cleary of the Australian Broadcasting Corporation reflected on that occasion as follows:

'I heard a noise and looked around and coming

down the road was one thing you dread when you're in that situation, a convoy of Casspirs, the big armoured vehicles with machine guns on top. You know they're loaded with police and teargas, and you think, "What is going to happen now?" By this time the other bishops had moved out of their cars and were pressing through the crowd. I could no longer see them but I heard the archbishop say, "Let us pray". Then the noise of the vehicles stopped. The crowd went quiet. There was no sound from the Casspirs, no sound of teargas canisters. So I looked around and there behind me were the Anglican bishops of southern Africa – black, white, coloured, old, young – standing between the crowd and the Casspirs, with their arms outstretched. In that moment I understood a little about what the Christian vision for a new South Africa cost people. I'd never witnessed that sort of courage before.'

It is this spirit of bold defiance in pursuit of justice that Tutu was more instrumental than anyone in encouraging, both in South Africa and among those who supported the fight to end apartheid further afield. Tutu's religiously inspired stance on questions of justice earned him critics over the years, yet never deterred him from following that calling. In a long career as arguably the foremost figure in the fight to end apartheid after the government banned the African National Congress, the 'Arch' as he is known by many, continues to pursue his relentless duty to justice across the globe and in South Africa. He has been instrumental in pioneering an approach to bringing about difficult political transitions that continues to hold out the promise of more peaceful resolutions.

For those familiar – and less familiar – with the struggle that ended apartheid in South Africa, the words of Archbishop Desmond Mpilo Tutu collected here promise to provide inspiration in confronting challenges of discrimination and moral uncertainty which we all face, individually or collectively.

David Shepherd

On African Churches

You are here to remind the church that
whenever it is obedient to this Lord and
Master, the church will end up, as its Lord
and Master, on the Cross. Because when the
church speaks out on behalf of the weak and
the poor, the powerful and the rich don't like
it. A church that does not suffer is not the
Church of Jesus Christ.

I believe fervently that the church is going to
be the salvation of Africa. If the church fails,
then I am frightened for the future.

> *Writing in the late 1970s about the*
> *numerous developmental and political*
> *problems Tutu witnessed in then Zaire as*
> *an employee of the Theological Education*
> *Fund.*

It pains me to have to admit that there is
less freedom and personal liberty in most of
independent Africa than there was during the
much-maligned colonial days. The Gospel of
Jesus Christ cannot allow us to keep silent
in the face of this ... We must be committed
to the total liberation of God's children,

politically, socially, economically.

At the Fifth All Africa Conference of Churches in 1987 Tutu was frank about what it meant to be a witness for Christ in Africa.

God is a God who sides with the hungry and the poor and the marginalised, and so we are able to tell the powerful everywhere, we tell the oppressor everywhere ... 'Watch it! Watch it! Watch it! Because God comes to deliver!'

On The African National Congress

The Bible and the Church predates Marxism and the African National Congress by several centuries.

There were those in the ranks of the ANC who were a great deal more incensed [about my comments about their having joined the government gravy train vacated by the apartheid regime]. Those who do find it a little difficult to live with criticism. And one worries about that. That there are those of them who don't actually recognise people who are basically on their side, who are critical, not because they want to see them fail. It is precisely the opposite. It is to say we want to see you succeed, and that is why we mention these things.

Referring to the reaction by the ANC to the official findings of the Truth and Reconciliation Commission (TRC) in 1994.

What an unedifying spectacle the leadership contest has become. Cry, the beloved country, cry as we see more and more who thumb their noses at the people. Those choosing party leaders – please do not choose those who will make us hang our heads in shame.

Tutu wrote to the Mail & Guardian *in 2007 ostensibly warning the nation of worrying developments he felt were afoot.*

On African Theology

The African would understand perfectly well what the Old Testament meant when it said 'man belongs to the bundle of life', that he is not a solitary individual. He is linked backwards to the ancestors whom he reveres, and forward with all the generations to be born. How do you speak about a God who loves you, a redeemer, a saviour, when you live like an

animal? ... Is the training given in the often
sheltered ivory towers at all geared to speak
relevantly to this and similar situations? ... It is
a whole philosophy and lifestyle in theological
education that must be revolutionised.

On Anger

Without forgiveness, there's no future.

The act of telling one's story has a cathartic,
healing effect.

On the Anglican Church

It really has no reason to exist in a world
that is so fissiparous, yet it does ... The
Anglican Communion continues to baffle all
outsiders, because it is a family with all the
tensions and differences, loves and hates,
squabbles and agreements that characterise
a family. Yes, we have the peculiar Anglican
genius for accommodating all kinds of views
in this extraordinary attribute called our
comprehensiveness.

*Reflecting on the 1978 Lambeth Conference
entitled 'What is the Church for?'*

Our world is facing problems – poverty, HIV and Aids – a devastating pandemic – and conflict. God must be weeping looking at some of the atrocities that we commit against one another. In the face of all of that, our church, especially the Anglican Church, at this time is almost obsessed with questions of human sexuality.

> *In a 2007 interview with BBC 4 Tutu criticised the 70-million-strong institution's attitude toward the issue of homosexuality.*

I'm speechless and I guess there are some who would prefer me to remain that way!

> *His immediate reaction when elected as Archbishop of Cape Town in 1986, to those outside awaiting the result.*

On Apartheid

Do you recall how police would climb trees in order to peep into bedrooms, hoping to catch out couples who might be contravening the Immorality Act, rushing to feel the temperature of the sheets, making sordid what should have been beautiful love between two persons, and how many careers and lives were destroyed when

people faced charges under this abominable
legislation?

> *Tutu – not without his characteristic eye for*
> *the absurd – reminds the audience of the past*
> *in setting about detailing the achievements of*
> *the country since then, during his delivery of*
> *the second Nelson Mandela Annual Lecture,*
> *2004, organised by the Nelson Mandela*
> *Foundation.*

For goodness' sake, will they hear, will white
people hear what we are trying to say? Please,
all we are asking you to do is to recognise that
we are humans, too.
1985

I stopped being a teacher when the South
African government introduced a deliberately
inferior education for blacks called Bantu
education, and I felt I wasn't ready to
collaborate with this apology for an edu-
cational system. Our children, the 1976 kids
who revolted against apartheid in Soweto,
called it 'gutter education', and it was gutter
education.

Apartheid is an evil as immoral and un-
Christian in my view as Nazism, and in my

view, the Reagan administration's support and
collaboration with it is equally immoral, evil, and
totally unChristian, without remainder.

*Speaking in the United States Congress in
1984.*

I am black and there are many times when I
have asked whether God really cared for us
when I have looked at some things that our
people have suffered. When the South African
Defence Force raided Maputo and Maseru a
few years ago, we were told we could not hold
memorial services. I held such services because
I did not think then, nor do I think now, that I
can be told by a secular authority what services
I may or may not hold. They kill our children
and then prescribe how we may bury them and
they think we do not hurt. What do they think
happens to us? For them we are really less than
human, spoken of as 'those people'. Our pain,
our anguish, one day will burst forth in an
unstoppable flood.

I am quite angry. I think the West, for my part,
can go to hell.

*Speaking in 1986 about the description by
Western leaders, as they prevaricated in*

decisively denouncing apartheid leaders, of
freedom fighters as terrorists.

What do [my critics in the West] make of what
Our Lord said to the Pharisees? 'Generation of
vipers', 'You white sepulchres. You walk around
looking smart outside when you are rotten bones
inside.' And what of Paul? I mean, Paul says,
'I consign you to the devil.' He also said, 'He
who says Jesus is not Lord, let him be accursed.'
Well, saying the West can go to hell is no worse
than that!

You have lost! Let us say this nicely: You have
already lost! We are inviting you to come and
join the winning side! Your cause is unjust.
You are defending what is fundamentally
indefensible, because it is evil. It is evil without
question. It is immoral. It is immoral without
question. It is unChristian. Therefore you
will bite the dust! And you will bite the dust
comprehensively!

Toward the time of the final capitulation
of the apartheid regime Tutu continued to
fire up – here in 1988 – congregations with
rousing sermons.

I told [Minister of Police] Mr Vlok, 'You know you have lost.' I said it nice and quietly, I didn't shout like now. I said: 'You know you have lost, you know from your history. You believed you were being oppressed by the British, you fought against the British and in the end you became free. The lesson you must learn from your own history is that when people decide to be free, nothing, just nothing, absolutely nothing can stop them.'

It is right to point out the good things that the Nationalist government did so as to have a rounded picture. But I have to say that ultimately it is irrelevant whether racism or apartheid sometimes produced good results. Because the tree was bad the fruit also had to be bad. For me this is an article of faith.

On the Black Consciousness Movement

A new breed of blacks who have iron in their souls.

The Black Consciousness Movement is not a hate white movement, despite all you have heard to the contrary. [Steve Biko] had a far too profound respect for people as persons to want to deal with them under ready-made, shop-soiled categories.

On Black Economic Empowerment

What is black empowerment when it seems to benefit not the vast majority but an élite that tends to be recycled?

On Black Theology

Black theology has occurred mainly in South Africa, where blacks have had their noses rubbed in the dust by white racism, depersonalising them to the extent that they have – blasphemy of blasphemies – come to doubt the reality of their own personhood. They have come to believe that the denigration of their humanity by those who oppress them is the truth about themselves.

Black theology is not so naïve as to think that white oppression is the only bondage from which the blacks need to be liberated.

Black theology is an engaged, not an academic, detached theology. It has gut level theology, relating to real concerns, the life and death issues of the black man. Black theology seeks to make sense of the life experience of the black man ... it is to be concerned with the humanisation of man, because those who ravage our humanity dehumanise themselves in the process; [it says] that the liberation of the black man is the other side of the coin of the liberation of the white man – so it is concerned with human liberation.

Liberation theology becomes part of people's struggle for liberation; it tries to help victims of oppression to assert their humanity so they can look the other chap in the eye and speak face to face without shuffling their feet and apologising for their black existence.

On Black South Africans

The unnecessary and untold suffering that apartheid inflicted on many of God's children was not because a potentially good policy went awry, or that black family life was systematically undermined by the migratory labour system because of a mistake. It flowed from a basic premise that those at the receiving end of policy were not quite human as those who made laws for them, pushing them beyond their frontiers, into homelands or locations, into inferior schools and hospitals, unskilled jobs and segregated teams.

Oh God help us that when the whites have turned to loving, the blacks will not have turned to hating.

Reiterating a quote from Alan Paton's Cry the Beloved Country.

[They don't want] crumbs of concession from a generous master, they want to be at the table, planning the menu with him ... the name of the game is political power-sharing.

On Botho/Ubuntu

Africans believe in something that is difficult to render in English. We call it ubuntu or botho. It means the essence of being human. It speaks about humaneness, gentleness, hospitality, putting yourself out on behalf of others, being vulnerable. It embraces compassion and toughness. It recognises that my humanity is bound up with yours, for we can only be human together.

Without this quality a prosperous man, even though he might be a chief, was regarded as someone deserving of pity and sometimes even contempt.

On His Childhood

I was not particularly politically conscious and I even thought that the racist ordering of affairs was something divinely ordained ... I remember so vividly accompanying my schoolteacher father to town and how sorry I felt for him when he would almost invariably be stopped and asked peremptorily and rudely to produce his 'exemption' [permitting him some leeway due to his schoolteacher status] in the street.

On Children

Children are a wonderful gift ... They have an extraordinary capacity to see into the heart of things and to expose sham and humbug for what they are.

It is drummed into our heads, from our most impressionistic days, that you must grind the opposition into the dust. We get so worked up that our children can become nervous wrecks as they are egged on to greater efforts by competitive parents.

A rebellious child is really testing out the parameters of acceptable conduct, and that is part of the painful process of growing up.

On His Children

I see myself in Trevor. Some of the weaker me, when it has surfaced in him, has made me more angry with him because I was angry with myself.

My wife and I decided early on in our marriage that we were going to try to let our children do a lot of things we had been denied in our childhood. We had been brought up to know that children are meant to be seen and not heard. As children we used to feel so terribly frustrated when these gods of our household –

our parents and their grown-up friends – were discussing something really interesting. We were burning to ask 'who' or 'what' in order to clarify some obscure point, but we never dared to interrupt … My wife and I did not want our children to go through all those traumas … We stuck it out very painfully. We let them join in discussions with our adult friends – they interrupted, they argued, they contributed. We discovered there was much fun in the home, and we parents developed as we pitted our strengths against those of the children. They were persons in their own right, and we had to think out many things that previously we had taken for granted.

On Christians

We expect them to reflect the character of Jesus Christ. We expect Christians to be gentle, not always quarrelling and scratching. We expect Christians to be humble as Jesus was humble … But we also expect Christians to stand up for justice … and when that happens then Christians will be trustworthy, believable witnesses.

On Christianity

Why should you need Marxist ideology, or
whatever? The Bible is dynamite ... Nothing
could be more radical.

We must each share in Calvary and the Cross
for only so can we share in the glory of the
Resurrection.

The Christian faith has been responsible for
some of the most horrendous atrocities and we
who are Christians ought to be a great deal more
modest.

Jesus Christ for me is the full and final
revelation of God. I will not compromise my
belief in His absolute uniqueness.

On the Church

The church is the fellowship whence adoration,
worship and praise ascend to the heavenly
throne and in company with the angels and
archangels and with the whole host of heaven
we sing as did the cherubic choir in Isaiah's

vision, and as we shall soon be bidden to do in his glorious service: 'Holy, Holy, Holy, Lord God of Hosts, heaven and earth are full of thy glory.'

It is from these remarkable men [the Fathers of the Community of the Resurrection] that I learned that it is impossible for religion to be sealed off in a watertight compartment that has no connection with the hurly burly business of ordinary living.

It is a great comfort to know that one need only throw oneself into this current and be borne by it and upheld by it ... It is wonderful to belong to the Church of God.

On the Church's Agenda

Liberation from sin in all its manifestations, liberation to be all that God wants his children to be.

On Colonialism

The colonial powers have often kept together

what should have been separated and separated
what should have been kept united – with
continuing repercussions in today's Africa.

We had the land, they had the Bible. Then they
said, 'Let us pray' and we closed our eyes. When
we opened them again, they had the land and
we had the Bible. Maybe we had the better deal.

I was teaching as if I was teaching people
in Europe, really ... I wasn't as abrasive as
I should have been considering what was
happening just across the road in Fort Hare.
And what was happening in the country.
I'm amazed now at how innocent in some
ways I was.

> *Tutu recounts teaching at the Anglican
> Federal Theological Seminary in South
> Africa after completing his theological
> training in the United Kingdom in the
> 1960s.*

The colonial countries really exploited their
colonies and fed back very little of the wealth
they bled from these countries. Poverty stares
you in the face.

On Communication

Let us watch our tongues. We can hurt, we
can extinguish a weak flickering light by harsh
words ... It is easy to discourage; it is far too
easy, all too easy to criticise, complain, to
rebuke. Let us try instead to be more quick to
see even a small amount of good in a person and
concentrate on that. Let us be more quick to
praise than to find fault. Let us be more quick
to thank others than complain – 'Thank you'
and 'Please' are small words, but they are oh, so
powerful.

On Communism

When Cape Town marched, not only South
Africa followed but much of Europe as well.
They marched in Eastern Europe and the Berlin
Wall fell. Autocratic communist regimes fell
and Mr Gorbachev carried out a more radical
revolution than that of 1917 with little loss of
life ... Praise be to God.

> *Part of an ecstatic letter written to*
> *Capetonians upon Mandela's 1990 release*
> *from prison.*

On Corporal Punishment

Millions of the world's children still suffer
from humiliating acts of violence, and these
violations of their rights as human beings can
have serious and lifelong effects. Violence begets
violence and we shall reap a whirlwind. Children
can be disciplined without violence that instils
fear and misery.

On Culture

The Third World must develop its own style
geared to its own needs and maybe we could still
teach others a thing or two.

On Darfur

[In speaking on behalf of the victims of the
political violence in Darfur, we, The 'Elders']
want community leaders in Darfur to feel
that they have been heard by us. And to the
extent that we could then communicate their
aspirations, their longings, particularly the
women's groups, we will do so.

Our hope is that we can keep Darfur in the spotlight and spur on governments to help keep peace in the region.

On the Death Sentence

I am delighted that the death penalty is being removed from the globe.

On Democracy

Vigorous debate, dissent, disagreements and discussion ... no one is infallible ... No government can be God.

My father used to say, 'Improve your argument, don't raise your voice.'

> *Final word of advice on the topic of engagement in democracy, during Tutu's 2008 Dullah Omar Memorial Lecture at the University of the Western Cape.*

There surely can't have been unanimity from the outset. I did not agree with [President Mbeki] but that did not make me his enemy. He knows that I hold him in high regard but none of us is infallible, and that is why we are a democracy and not a dictatorship.

From Tutu's 2004 Nelson Mandela Lecture.

National governments may have admirable
policies and even budget for their implemen-
tation, but if they do not get implemented at
the local level then they are as good as non-
existent. Central and second-tier governments
can talk until they are blue in their faces about
their splendid policies, but unless the people at
the coalface of life experience them through
service delivery it is all vanity of vanities, as the
Good Book says in Ecclesiastes.

We should not impugn the motives of others
but accept the bona fides of all. If we believe
in something, then surely we will be ready to
defend it rationally, hoping to persuade those
opposed to change their point of view?

On Determination

All of us have some inadequacy or other. We
prove our maturity by how we deal with that
fact. Most of us pretend we don't and throw our
weight around to prove that we count.

Many in the black community ask why I still waste my time talking to whites and I tell them that our mandate is biblical. Moses went to the Pharaoh several times even when he knew it was futile. The prophets addressed the kings of Israel time and again because theirs was to deliver the message faithfully even if they were being rejected.

> *Tutu again contextualised the struggle for justice, this time in the late 1970s during a period of growing frustration.*

On Education

Apartheid has spawned discriminatory education, such as Bantu Education, education for serfdom, ensuring that the government spends only one tenth on one black child per annum for education what it spends on a white child ... It is to be wantonly wasteful of human resources, because so many of God's children are prevented, by deliberate government policy, from attaining their fullest potential. South Africa is paying a heavy price already for this iniquitous policy because there is a desperate shortage of skilled manpower ... In this matter, the South African government and its supporters are being properly hoisted with their own petard.

From his Nobel Prize speech, 1984.

Our education faces serious problems. Bantu education has left us a pernicious legacy. We should help teachers recover their morale.

Observation and appeal made during Tutu's 2008 Dullah Omar Memorial Lecture at the University of the Western Cape.

On Forgiveness

Revenge is contrary to the spirit of ubuntu/botho. To forgive reflects the generosity of this ubuntu/botho.

A lamb will hardly stray from its mother. It is the troublesome, obstreperous sheep which is likely to go astray, going through the fence, having its wool torn and probably ending up in a ditch of dirty water. It is this dirty, smelling, riotous creature which the Good Shepherd goes after, leaving the good, well-behaved 99 sheep in the wilderness and He finds it, why He carries it on His shoulder and calls His friends to celebrate with Him.

Let us blacks not be filled with hatred and bitterness. For all of us, black and white together, shall overcome, indeed have already overcome.

> *Speaking in 1977 at the memorial service of slain Black Consciousness leader, Steve Biko.*

The parents of the murdered Fulbright scholar, Amy Biehl, who campaigned at Stanford University in the anti-apartheid campaign, and was murdered as she gave a lift to student friends to Gugulethu township when she was an exchange student in Cape Town, were obviously shattered, yet instead of being embittered and seeking revenge they did not oppose the amnesty applications of those who killed their child so brutally. They attended the amnesty hearings and supported the entire process of reconciliation and amnesty. They embraced the families of the murderers of their child and they have established the Amy Biehl Foundation to rescue as many as possible of Gugulethu's youth from the dead ends that might well be their lot.

Revenge and retribution are easy, being the path of least resistance. Forgiveness is not for sissies. Our Scriptures declare that it is an attribute that makes us Godlike.

On God

He has shown Himself to be a doing God.
Perhaps we might add another point about
God – He takes sides. He is not a neutral God.
He took the side of the slaves, the oppressed,
the victims. He does not sleep or go on holiday
or take a day off. He is always there. So don't
despair.

God does not permit us to dwell in a kind
of spiritual ghetto; insulated from real
life ... Jesus refused to remain on the Mount
of Transfiguration, but descended to the
valley beneath to be involved with healing the
possessed boy.

On HIV/Aids

We defeated apartheid; this is a scourge we can
also defeat. Please, let us all be galvanised and
fight the scourge.

We as churches have an opportunity to tell
people that Aids is not God's punishment for
sin. If it was, we should ask ourselves what has

a new-born baby who has contracted the disease done?

On Homosexuality

We struggled against apartheid in South Africa, supported by people the world over, because black people were being blamed and made to suffer for something we could do nothing about; our very skins ... It is the same with sexual orientation. It is a given.

If God as they say is homophobic I wouldn't worship that God.

The Jesus I worship is not likely to collaborate with those who vilify and persecute an already oppressed minority.

It's like saying you choose to be black in a race-infected society.

Why should we want all homosexual persons not to give expression to their sexuality in loving acts? Why don't we use the same criteria to judge same-sex relationships that we use to judge whether heterosexual relationships are whole or not?

On Humanity

We human beings, ever since the Garden of Eden, are looking for scapegoats. We remain children of Adam and Eve, and have the genes for looking for excuses.

On the Iraq War

There is one magnanimous act the new president could make. The new president would be surprised by the world's reaction if he were to say, 'We made a big mistake over Iraq. We're sorry.'

Tutu delivered the 2007 Warren and Anita Manshel Lecture in American Foreign Policy at Harvard's Weatherhead Centre for International Affairs.

On Jesus Christ

Jesus affirms me and says I matter ... so I can have a proper self-assurance. You know how we all blossom in the presence of one who sees the good in us and who can coax the best out of us ... Just note how Jesus was able to get a prostitute like Mary Magdalene to become one of the greatest saints. He mentioned the quality in her which nobody else noticed – her great capacity to love, and from selling her body she became one of His most loyal followers.

On Justice

The word of God calls His people to work for justice, for only thus can there be peace.

On Leadership

A leader is there for the sake of the led.

On His Life

If it weren't for faith I would have given up long ago.

I did notice [the different treatment of black South Africans], but I can't pretend that I was aware it was going to make an indelible impression on me. It was only much later when Dr Verwoerd introduced the deliberately inferior education for blacks and stopped the free school meals which had been introduced in some black schools that my boyhood memories were revived.

I had wanted to become a physician and I was admitted to medical school but my family couldn't afford the fees, so I went into teaching. And almost always when I go to, say, Groote Schuur [Hospital] and I see these young people with their stethoscopes, I have a small little part of me that longs for a time when I could have had a stethoscope. But, ja, that's a longing that I've had, but as a second option I've had a very good life, really, very fulfilling.

As you can see, I'm not exactly young. One of the benefits of not being young is that you are permitted to repeat yourself, and so if you have heard this story before, be nice to an old decrepit man and laugh.

> *Speaking at the Minneapolis Convention Center as part of the You-thrive PeaceJam Conference promoting peace among young people in 2008.*

I am a leader by default, only because nature does not allow a vacuum.

They must not be angry with God and pull out of the church. They must rather try to change my views ... I am me! I operate in the way Desmond Tutu operates. I don't sit down and work out strategies. I operate almost instinctively. As I believe the Gospel demands.

Addressing concerns critics had about his appointment as Archbishop of Cape Town in 1986.

There is nothing the government can do to me that will stop me from being involved in what I believe is what God wants me to do. I do not do it because I like doing it. I do it because I am under what I believe to be the influence of God's hand. I cannot help it. I cannot help it when I see injustice. I cannot keep quiet. I will not keep quiet, for, as Jeremiah says, when I try to keep quiet God's word burns like a fire in my breast. But what is it that they can ultimately do? The most awful thing that they can do is to kill me, and death is not the worst thing that can happen to a Christian.

Part of Tutu's testimony during the 1982

Commission of Enquiry into the South
African Council of Churches.

On Marriage

What heinous crime have these women
committed, to be hounded like criminals in
this manner? All they wanted is to be with
their husbands, the fathers of their children.
Everywhere else in the world they would be
highly commended, but in South Africa, a land
that claims to be Christian and that boasts a
public holiday called Family Day, these gallant
women are treated so inhumanely, and yet all
they want is to have a decent and stable family
life. It is part of the price human beings, God's
children, are called to pay for apartheid. An
unacceptable price.

> *Tutu's daughter, Naomi, recalled words*
> *of her father in one of his appeals to the*
> *conscience of the country's leaders in her*
> *1988 collection of her father's thoughts.*

On Men

Men almost always give the impression that
they are the bosses, especially at home, but all

the while they know who the real bosses are. Many are described as male chauvinist pigs really only because they are trying to bolster their sagging morale by throwing their weight around, or at least trying to do so.

On the Situation in the Middle East

My wife and I with our two young children stayed for two months in Jerusalem in 1966 and we saw the escalating violence and the mounting tensions between Jew and Arab which preceded the Six Day War.

God, this happened to [South Africa], we pray for those who made it happen. Forgive them. Help us forgive and help us so that we in our turn will not make others suffer.

How people with your kind of history could allow the government of Israel, as distinct from the people, to have the kind of relationship with the government of South Africa that it has ... we cannot understand how Jews can cooperate with a government many of whose members were sympathetic to Hitler and the Nazis. Whether Jews [accuse me of anti-semitism] or not, I will continue to be highly critical of Israel in this regard.

> *In a 1989 visit to New York Tutu praised opposition from within Israel to strong arm government actions, including massacres in Lebanese refugee camps, appealing for the widening of such action.*

The church must be ready to speak the truth in love. It has a responsibility for all, the rich and the poor, the ruler and the ruled, the oppressed and the oppressor, but it needs to point out that God does take sides. Incredibly, he sides with those whom the world would marginalise, whom the world considers of little account. That was what he did in founding Israel. He took their side when they did not deserve it against the powerful, against Pharaoh. That was a paradigmatic act that gave an important clue about the sort of God he is.

You have been a tremendous light to the world. We are proud to acknowledge the riches of our Jewish heritage.

I am Christian, many of the Palestinians are Christians, in fact many are Anglicans, and their anguish tears my heart apart.

But we say also, dear brothers and sisters, the Jews have a right to their independent state as well.

[The situation in Israel] is a shattering experience and the world must never forget our inhumanity to one another.

If you changed the names, the description of what is happening in the Gaza Strip and the West Bank could be a description of what is happening in South Africa ... Israel cannot do that. It is out of line with her biblical and historical traditions.

> *Tutu reiterated his feeling that a comparison between Israel policies toward the Palestinians and those of apartheid South Africa was warranted in a 1989 visit to New York, where he spoke at the Stephen Wise Free Synagogue.*

God has a special caring for those whom the world thinks are not important ... God sides

with those whom the world despises ...
God sides with those whom the world
brutalises ... God is with those whom it
oppresses.

People are scared in this country [the United
States]; to say wrong is wrong because the pro-
Israel lobby is powerful – very powerful. Well,
so what? For goodness' sake, this is God's world!
We live in a moral universe. The apartheid
government was very powerful, but today it no
longer exists. Hitler, Mussolini, Stalin, Pinochet,
Milosevic, and Idi Amin were all powerful, but
in the end they bit the dust.

> *In 2002 Tutu addressed an 'Ending the*
> *Occupation' conference in Boston.*

In Jerusalem in 1999 there really was a deep
interest in the process of the Truth and
Reconciliation Commission and in the concept
of forgiveness and reconciliation. I was able to
point out that we had learned in South Africa
that true security would never be won through
the barrel of a gun. True security would come
when all inhabitants of the Middle East, that
region so revered by many, believed that their
human rights and dignity were respected and

upheld, when true justice prevailed. I had not changed my own points of view: I still felt there was a need for forgiveness and that there ought to be security for the State of Israel and justice and equity for the Palestinians. But somehow in Israel I was seen in a new light.

> *Reflecting on a 1989 visit to the Yad Vashem Holocaust Museum in Jerusalem, where he had raised the issue of forgiveness and met with little resonance, but sensed a change in attitudes in a return visit in 1999.*

One reason we succeeded in South Africa that is missing in the Middle East today is the quality of leadership – leaders willing to make unpopular compromises, to go against their own constituencies, because they have the wisdom to see that would ultimately make peace possible.

On Morality

Do your little bit of good where you are; it's those little bits of good put together that overwhelm the world.

On Myanmar

I think we ought to celebrate the incredible
courage of our sisters and brothers in Burma.
It is incumbent on us to say no – please, for
goodness' sake, listen to the calls of the people.
The people are saying we just want freedom and
democracy.

2007

On the South African Negotiated Settlement

Thank you for the courage of those who
initiated change. Thank you O God for those
who sacrificed their freedom and even their
lives in the struggle for justice. Thank you for
bringing those who were previously enemies
around the same table to achieve a negotiated
settlement.

*At Nelson Mandela's presidential
inauguration.*

On Negotiation

Negotiations are not things that happen
between friends. They happen between enemies,

especially the ones you can't stand ... if you want peace, you speak to the people you find most unacceptable.

On Receiving the 1984 Nobel Peace Prize

The award of the Nobel Prize is a tremendous political statement. It says that despite all the distortion of truth, the world recognises that we are striving for peace. It is a tremendous affirmation that our cause is just and methods are praiseworthy.

It is our prize. It is not Desmond Tutu's prize. The world recognises that, and thank God that our God is God. I want to thank the Nobel Committee; I want to thank the churches of Norway and everywhere for their support, their love, their prayers. On behalf of all these for whom you have given new hope, a cause for joy, I want to accept this award in a wholly representative capacity.

A new hope has been kindled in the breast of millions who are voiceless, oppressed, dispossessed, tortured by the powerful tyrants, lacking elementary human rights in Latin America, South East Asia, the Far East, in many parts of Africa and behind the Iron Curtain, who have had their noses rubbed in the dust.

If God be for us who can be against us?

On Non-racialism

One day I was standing in the street with my mother when a white man in a priest's clothing walked past. As he passed us he took off his hat to my mother. I couldn't believe my eyes – a white man who greeted a black working class woman!

[Appointing white priests in black townships is important] to dispel any erroneous notions which people may have picked up in having unfortunate dealings only with the police, the army and a phalanx of bureaucrats who have the unenviable task of applying evil and unChristian policies.

How I pray that Our Lord would open our eyes so that we would see the real, the true identity of each one of us, that this is not a so-called 'coloured', or white, or black or Indian, but a brother, a sister – and treat each other as such. Would you let your brother live an unnatural life as a migrant worker in a single-sex hostel?

You would have thought by this time [black people] would be saying, 'To hell with all white people.' They say, 'Ah-ha we don't hate white people, we hate apartheid, we hate injustice, we hate oppression and we are for goodness, for justice and for peace … We are going to stride into this great future, this new South Africa, this non-racial South Africa where people will count not because of the colour of their skins, but where people count because they have been made in the image of God.'

> *At a 1987 funeral of a white activist where most of the 20 000 attendees were black.*

[At his release in 1990, Mandela] said he really was amazed as he came out of Victor Verster [Prison], and was even more amazed at the fact that it was multiracial, with so many white people ... he was over the moon, but he was also genuinely quite taken aback.

On Northern Ireland

Don't let any feel they have been left out. Any group, however small, which has grievances, real or imaginary, must not feel excluded; otherwise you can kiss goodbye to peace. Let them be represented by those regarded as their authentic spokespersons.

On Oppression

When two persons are engaged in a conflict and one of them is considerably stronger than the other, to be neutral is not just and fair and impartisan because to be neutral is in fact to side with the powerful.

If detention without trial is evil in South Africa then it must be evil in every part of the African continent.

Yesterday's oppressed can quite easily become tomorrow's oppressors.

Reacting to the controversial attempt by
ANC president Thabo Mbeki to prevent
from becoming public the final Truth and
Reconciliation Commission Report in 1998
because it found the ANC guilty of gross
human rights violations in its treatment of
detainees in its armed camps in Angola.

This is a moral universe. Right and wrong
actually do matter. Ultimately, truth, justice,
goodness and compassion will triumph over
their ghastly counterparts.

On Peace

If we want peace ... let us work for justice. Let
us beat our swords into ploughshares.

Because there is global insecurity, nations
are engaged in a mad arms race, spending
billions of dollars wastefully on instruments of
destruction, when millions are starving. Just a
fraction of what is expended so obscenely on
defence budgets would make the difference in
enabling God's children to fill their stomachs, be
educated, and given the chance to lead fulfilled
and happy lives.

Economists Allied for Arms Reduction
(ECAAR) has my full support.

> *ECAAR is an organisation based in*
> *America that campaigns for disarmament.*

On People

Each person is not just to be respected but to
be revered as one created in God's image. To
treat anyone as if they were less than this is
not just evil, not just painful – it is veritably
blasphemous, for it is to spit in the face of God.

On Personalities

Steve Biko, Black Consciousness Movement leader killed while in police custody

Steve has started something that is quite
unstoppable. The powers of evil, of injustice,
of oppression, of exploitation have done their
worst and they have lost.

Let us praise and bless God for giving us such a
priceless gift as Steve. Yes, it is a priceless gift
which in one sense South Africa has wasted

wantonly as our beloved country has done so scandalously in the past and continues to do. God called Steve Biko to be his servant in South Africa – to speak up on behalf of God, declaring what the will of this God must be in a situation such as ours, a situation of evil, injustice, oppression and exploitation.

Steve saw, more than most of us, just how injustice and oppression can dehumanise and make us all, black and white, victim and oppressor alike, less than what God intended us to be.

PW Botha, Former State President

I don't know whether that is how Jesus would have handled it. But at that moment I didn't actually quite mind how Jesus would have handled it. I was going to handle it my way.

> During a shouting match in 1988 between Archbishop Tutu and the then State President, Tutu ended up waving his finger in Botha's face – as Botha was notorious for doing from various podiums – as a torrent of insults was unleashed between the two men, saying 'Look here, I'm not a small boy. Don't think you're talking to a small boy. I'm not here as if you're my principal ... I thought I

45

was talking to a civilised person and there are
courtesies involved.'

Whether I like it or not, whether he likes it or
not ... PW Botha is my brother and I must
desire and pray for the best for him.

If Mr Botha was able to say: I am sorry that
the policies of my government caused you pain.
Just that. Can he bring himself to say I am
sorry that the policies of my government caused
you so much pain? That would be a tremendous
thing and I appeal to him.

> *One of the statements Tutu made in giving*
> *evidence against P. W. Botha at South*
> *Africa's TRC.*

I tried to reach out to Mr Botha. God did
not call me to be a pastor of black people,
God called me to be a pastor of his children.
Mr Botha is my brother because that is the
interpretation of my faith and my baptism. He
is a member of my family, and God will ask me,
'What did you do to help redeem my child?'

FW de Klerk, former State President

We were listened to.

*On De Klerk's greater willingness to consult
on some matters when he took over as South
Africa's State President from PW Botha in
1989.*

There was an avalanche of information. To say I
did not know ... I find that hard to understand.
I have got to say that I sat there [presiding
at the Truth and Reconciliation Commission
(TRC)] and I was close to tears. I feel sorry for
him. I am devastated.

*In 1997 Tutu was distressed to find that the
ex-President pleaded ignorance of apartheid
atrocities uncovered by human rights groups.*

Chris Hani, assassinated general secretary of the South African Communist Party

There are so very many occasions when it did
seem it was touch and go and none more terrible
than the assassination of Chris Hani. That was
one of the scariest moments in our lives for most
of us. We were a whisker's breadth away from
total catastrophe.

*Tutu reminds an audience of South Africa's
recent past in setting about detailing the
achievements of the country since then,
during his delivery of the second Nelson*

Mandela Annual Lecture, 1994, organised by the Nelson Mandela Foundation.

I loved Chris very, very deeply, and it was one of the most devastating moments and the anger was palpable. Had [Mandela] not gone on television and radio ... our country would have gone up in flames ... Because it would have been the easiest thing just to release the dogs of war. That is what maybe many of the younger Turks had wanted to see happen. Mercifully, he was there and held them all at bay.

Nelson Mandela

[His is] a legacy not just for South Africa. When you go round the world now, especially in the aftermath of the Truth and Reconciliation Commission, people do actually look at South Africa and see it as a sign of hope ... that will be his greatest achievement apart from having achieved, with all of the people, the liberation of South Africa.

Friends, this is the day that the Lord has made and we will rejoice and be glad in it. This is the day that we have waited for, for over 300 years.

This is the day of liberation for all of us, black and white together. Fellow South Africans, I ask you: welcome our brand-new State President, out-of-the-box, Nelson Mandela!

> *On 9 May 1994, after the first seating of democratically elected national legislature, Tutu introduced the public to President Mandela at a public celebration at Cape Town's Grand Parade.*

As a theologian, I would say ... we would say conventionally that he had disappeared, that this was a waste. That is how we all felt. This is a waste. This good man. It turns out, actually, that [his imprisonment] wasn't a waste. He was growing in depth ... And then God must have special kind of humour ... because I don't know when it got to happen that [Mandela] came to be a symbol for many, especially young people. It was spine tingling, actually, when you saw how people kept saying, 'Release Nelson Mandela' and meaning really, 'Release all of our political prisoners.'

There were some in the ANC who were sympathetic to the option taken by those organisations seeking to appear more radical than the ANC at the time of the negotiated settlement. Mr Mandela had to contend with these people. It required a great deal of political courage, skill and authority to bring his organisation along with him.

When [people] encounter a good person, they become reverent. Because we are actually made for that goodness, and there is an excitement that people have to see it embodied.

It is genuine, his care for the people. I mean that's where you hit him in the solar plexus. That isn't something that he puts on. It may come from the fact that he comes from a royal family. That even at that point, he was aware that he bears a particular responsibility. If his people are going to be prosperous, he's got to be a good chief, and a chief is a chief through the people ... It is a deep compassion which includes, as we have seen, those who have roughed him up.

When you hear some of his utterances before going to jail on the subject of violence, for instance, you are aware that a transformation happened. That he was not the fire-eater 27 years later that he had been, which doesn't

mean that he couldn't, for instance, get very
angry. Because there were flashes of the kind of
anger that he could have. I mean, when he gave
[then President] De Klerk that dressing down at
[the multiparty negotiating forum] CODESA.
He could feel a very deep anger. But I think
what happened to him in prison was something
that you have to now accept my authority for
it, that suffering can do one of two things to
a person. It can make you bitter and hard and
really resentful of things. Or as it seems to
do with very many people – it is like fires of
adversity that toughen someone. They make
you strong but paradoxically also they make
you compassionate, and gentle. I think that that
is what happened to him.

The one weakness that I would say is part of
his trend, it's this thing of seeing himself as a
member of the ANC. And having got used to
it in prison ... operating by consensus, that he
would probably find that it was difficult to move
on his own. He would have wanted to ensure
that the group came along with him. I would
say that there were times when I would have
hoped that he could have come out and said
very clearly and firmly, 'This is what we do.'

But then we would be encouraging a sort of dictatorial streak. I don't know. But there are times when you hoped for a greater definiteness.

In an interview with John Carlin in 1994.

It is, in fact, when he is released from the text and he speaks off the cuff that he lights up. I wish he could do that more often – just chuck away the text, or change his speech writer.

I fondly thought that Madiba was my friend and so, like a good friend, I told him I wasn't impressed with his sartorial taste and his penchant for these gaudy shirts. Do you know how he treated this friendly advice? Well, he retorted, 'That's pretty thick coming from a man who wears a dress in public.' Now can you beat it?

One of the opening remarks during Tutu's delivery of the occasion of the 2004 second Nelson Mandela Annual Lecture, organised by the Nelson Mandela Foundation. The exchange Tutu refers to came on the back of a more serious confrontation between the two over Tutu publicly criticising the new ANC government about not closing the apartheid era arms industry.

Winnie Madikizela Mandela, activist and former wife of Nelson Mandela

I still embrace you because I love you and I love you very deeply ... Say I am sorry; I am sorry for my part in what went wrong ... I beg you, I beg you, I beg you please.

> *Tutu at the 1997 TRC hearings, to which Ms Mandela offered a qualified apology for her role in criminal behaviour during the apartheid era.*

Thabo Mbeki, former State President of South Africa

Our country through President Thabo Mbeki has been in the forefront of the creation of the African Union and in the conception and promotion of NEPAD and the African Renaissance.

> *One, the many achievements of post-apartheid South Africa that Tutu listed on the occasion of the second Nelson Mandela Annual Lecture, organised by the Nelson Mandela Foundation.*

They would be so proud that their President [Mbeki] was playing such a prominent role in

Africa and elsewhere, especially with peace initiatives.

Speculating in 2007 about how those who had fought and died for the liberation of South Africa would feel were they alive today.

We are constantly castigating African presidents who want to be presidents for life. And I think the rejection of Thabo Mbeki going for a third time and somehow to ensconce himself as a president in perpetuity, is a good thing.

Many experience him as perhaps too English. He didn't carry his heart on his sleeve, as most of our people tend to do. He appeared to be aloof ... All of those factors militated against Thabo.

Robert Mugabe, long-time Zimbabwean President

I'm just devastated by what I can't explain, by what seems to be an aberration, this sudden change in character. But it does not in any way remove that he did do very well. Zimbabwe was for a very long time a showcase country.

[Robert Mugabe] did a fantastic job, and it's such a great shame, because he had a wonderful legacy. If he had stepped down ten or so years ago he would be held in very, very high regard.

2008

Barack Obama, President of the United States

He's a very astute person. And I think he has sought to find those next to him, near to him, who are more than competent. He's shown that in things like shutting down Guantánamo Bay and appointing George Mitchell as his special envoy to the Middle East. The signs are propitious ... But obviously, yes, maybe we could muck ourselves up by being unrealistic in our expectations.

Ronald Reagan, former President of the United States

He has really been saying blacks are expendable. He sits around in equanimity because the fatalities are black fatalities. I said he was a crypto-racist. I think I should say now he is a racist pure and simple.

In 1985 Tutu was quoted in the Washington

Post *in reference to his comments on Reagan's choice to support only limited sanctions.*

He sits there like the great white chief of old who could tell us black people that we don't know what is good for us, the white man knows.
New York Times, *1986*

Your president is the pits as far as blacks are concerned.

In July 1986 Tutu again rebuked Reagan after Reagan referred to sanctions as an 'historic act of folly'.

Somebody needs lessons in elementary history for surely nearly everybody ought to know that certainly in World War II many Afrikaners were opposed to fighting what they considered the Englishman's war. Whilst the Afrikaner especially hoped for a Nazi victory ... Black men risked their lives largely because they had been promised a new kind of society in the land of their birth after the war.

This remark followed comments at the height of the sanctions debate in the mid-1980s by President Reagan, that America should not abandon an old friend – apartheid South

Africa – who he claimed had unreproachfully fought side by side in many of the wars the US had been involved in.

Aung San Suu Kyi, Burmese pro-democracy campaigner

Please, please, how can men armed to the teeth be scared of this petite, demure, beautiful woman? We want to salute our sister Aung San Suu Kyi, who for 11 of the last 17 years is under house arrest. She's my only pin-up in my office.

Robert Sobukwe, founder of a 1959 breakaway political movement, the Pan Africanist Congress

He was already carrying out the tenets of the Black Consciousness movement long before anyone ever knew that there would be such a phenomenon as black consciousness.

The tragedy of this country is that its rulers refused to parley with such as Robert and they may regret missing that opportunity of negotiating radical change in South Africa peacefully.

'The Prof' was already thinking about other
people, hardly mentioning his agony.

> *Upon visiting the soon-to-die Sobukwe in
> hospital in 1978.*

Jacob Zuma, current President of South Africa

He's been inaugurated. He's appointed a new
cabinet. Let's see what happens. At this stage, I
am perhaps neutral ... I'm sad for my country. I
think we could have done a great deal better in
the way that we handled the differences ... But
then, politics is politics, and we have to live with
these realities as they are.

He's a very personable individual, warm and
very, very friendly and you can discuss with
him various things. But I'm still very unhappy
that his case was dealt with in the manner in
which it was dealt with. I don't have an animus
against him, it's the principle. For his own sake,
it should have been dealt with by a court.

> *In conversation with a journalist on Tutu's
> 78th birthday.*

I said that during his rape trial, when some of his supporters were saying quite unacceptable things against the woman who brought the charges against him, I would have thought that one would have remonstrated with them more forcefully than was the case.

On Political Activism

You are either on the side of the oppressed or on the side of the oppressor. You cannot be neutral.

How could I say no when they asked me to be part of a delegation to pressure the Burmese government to release Aung San Suu Kyi?

We are true witnesses if we are on the side of the weak, the powerless, and the exploited.

On Poverty

We can, many of us, make a difference by adopting a family to which we give a monthly gift of R100 or R200 – very few poor people want a handout; they are proud but they also need a leg up.

On Praise or Awards (for Himself)

I am standing out only because millions of my
compatriots are carrying me on their shoulders.

On Prayer

We are always in the presence of God. Prayer is
acknowledging that we are in that presence.

On the Priesthood

God grant to you the grace to be faithful in
prayer and study. I need not underline the
importance of faithfulness in pastoral work.
You can sit all day in your house and not visit
people, not take communion to the sick, to the
aged, and nobody will usually complain to you
but your church will grow emptier.

In our church here in South Africa, that doesn't
make a difference. We just say that at the
moment, we believe that they should remain
celibate and we don't see what the fuss is about.
*Defending his position on admitting gay
priests to the priesthood.*

On the Press

We have a free press which has proved to be a vigilant watchdog and an important institution of civil society. Sadly we cannot say the same about our public broadcaster, which has far too frequently been sycophantic and reminiscent of the SABC of old, so much an echo of His Master's Voice.

On Reconciliation

The chief work that Jesus came to perform on earth can be summed up in a word: 'Reconciliation' ... He came to restore human community and brotherhood which sin destroyed. He came to say that God had intended us for fellowship, for *koinonia*, for togetherness, without destroying our distinctiveness, our cultural otherness.

It is forgotten that reconciliation is no easy option, nor does it rule out confrontation. After all, it did cost God the death of His Son to effect reconciliation; the cross of Jesus was to expose the sinfulness of sin when he took on the powers of evil and routed them comprehensively.

Real reconciliation cost God the death of His Son and if we are to be instruments of His peace then we must know what we are about, that we must be ready to be marked with the cross of reconciliation, that we have to identify as our Lord identified, with the down and out, the drug addict, the homosexual, the prostitute, the poor and the downtrodden.

Forgiving and being reconciled are not about pretending that things are other than they are. It is not patting one another on the back and turning a blind eye to the wrong. True reconciliation exposes the awfulness, the abuse, the pain, the degradation, the truth. It could even make things worse. It is a risky undertaking, but in the end it is worthwhile, because in the end there will be real healing from having dealt with the real situation. Spurious reconciliation can bring about only spurious healing.

[Rugby] being so white and really so Afrikaner. And with everybody baying for the Springbok emblem to be destroyed, and that [Mandela] should come out wearing a Springbok jersey ... it was an electric moment. Quite unbelievable. It had the effect of just turning round our country ... it is unbelievable that when we won [the 1995 Rugby World Cup], people could be dancing in Soweto ... It said it is actually possible for us to become one nation. There was a great risk. It could have fallen flat on its face. They could have remembered him only as an uppity native ... Is it spontaneous? Is it calculated? The line is very thin.

I have wished desperately that those involved in seeking solutions for what have seemed intractable problems, in places such as Northern Ireland and the Middle East, would not despise the value of seemingly small symbolic gestures ... a small handshake can make the unthinkable, the improbable – peace, friendship, harmony and tolerance – not quite so remote.

Reconciliation is a long process. We don't have the kind of race clashes that we thought would happen. What we have is xenophobia, and it's very distressing. But maybe you ought to be lenient with us. We've been free for just 12 years.

On Religion

To ignore people of other faiths and ideologies
in an increasingly plural society is to be willfully
blind to what the Scriptures say about Christian
witness. We are severely impoverished if we
do not encounter people of other faiths with
reverence and respect for their belief and
integrity.

On His Retirement

I am still deeply longing for a quieter life. And
I really mean it when I say it. I'm really going
to try. My wife says that she's heard me say
that several times. I will try next year and be
ruthless. But what do you say when the prime
minister of the Solomon Islands writes and
says, please, could you come and be with us
when we launch our Truth and Reconciliation
Commission?

On the Sanctions Campaign to End Apartheid

Constructive engagement has worsened our
situation under apartheid ... It is giving

democracy a bad name, just as apartheid has
given free enterprise a bad name.

We ask you, please help us, urge the South
African authorities to go to the conference
table with the authentic sections of our
community ... Help us, that this freedom comes
for all of us in South Africa, black and white,
but that it comes with the least possible violence,
that it comes peacefully, that it comes soon.

On the Scriptures

Do [the Scriptures] say God is concerned only
about individual salvation and has no interest
in the redemption of the socio-political and
economic matrix in which individuals live?

On Society

Unless we work assiduously so that all of God's
children, our brothers and sisters, members of
one human family, all will enjoy basic human
rights, the right to a fulfilled life, the right of
movement, the freedom to be fully human,
within a humanity measured by nothing less

than the humanity of Jesus Christ Himself,
then we are on the road inexorably to self-
destruction, we are not far from global suicide
– and yet it could be so different.

Columbia is helping ... a university by definition
is a place where you have a whole plethora of
points of view.

> *On hearing that Columbia University*
> *was to host Iranian President Mahmoud*
> *Ahmadinejad in late 2007, so he could*
> *address students on campus.*

I want to say with all the circumspection and
deep sense of responsibility that I can muster,
that people can take only so much. As they say
in English, 'Even the worm will turn.' I have
seen too much violence in other parts of the
world to talk glibly about it, but I do want to
issue a serious warning, a warning that I am
distressed to have to make, and it is this: When
people are desperate then they will use desperate
methods.

> *Speaking at Steve Biko's funeral in 1977.*

I would hope [the G8] would begin to say, 'Let's
do something about subsidies.' I would hope
that people would realise that ultimately it is

in their own interest to begin to have a more equitable international economic system.

On Apartheid South Africa

I don't want to sound melodramatic, but it is extremely difficult being back here, having to ask permission from various white officials to visit my parents!

In a 1967 letter to an English friend.

You remember the story of the Zambian boasting to a South African about their minister of the navy. The South African scoffed: 'You are landlocked. How can you have a minister of the navy?' The Zambian retorted: 'Ah, but you claim to have a minister of justice.'

Ours is of course not a civil rights movement. You here were claiming what was guaranteed to you under your Constitution. The law was at least theoretically on your side. At home we are struggling for fundamental human rights and we are excluded by the Constitution from any meaningful participation in decision making. The law of the land is against us.

Speaking to an American audience in 1986.

We shall be free because our cause is a just cause. We do not want to dominate others; we just want to have our humanity acknowledged. Our freedom is not the gift of white people. They cannot decide to give or to withhold it. Our freedom is an inalienable right bestowed on us by God.

Mr de Klerk, please come here! We are inviting you, Mr de Klerk, we invite you Mr Vlok, we invite all the cabinet. We say, come, come here, can you see the people of this country? Come and see what this country is going to become. This country is a rainbow country! This country is technicolour. You can come and see the new South Africa!

> *Speaking to a crowd of 30 000 outside Cape Town City Hall in 1990, after the swearing in of FW de Klerk as State President following PW Botha's heart attack.*

By fighting and engaging in violent acts we give others the excuse to say we are not yet fit to govern ourselves.

> *Speaking during the transition to democracy when different political factions linked to ethnicity engaged in deadly violence.*

To the white community in general I say express
your commitment to change by agreeing to
accept a redistribution of wealth and a more
equitable sharing of the resources of the land.
Be willing to accept voluntarily a declension of
your very high standard of living. Isn't it better
to lose something voluntarily, and to assist in
bringing about change – political power sharing
– in an orderly fashion, rather than seeing this
come about through bloodshed and chaos, when
you stand to lose everything?

Yes indeed these people were guilty of
monstrous, even diabolical, deeds but that did
not turn them into monsters or demons. To
have done so would mean they could not be held
morally responsible for their dastardly deeds.
Monsters have no moral responsibility.

Once we have got it right, South Africa will be
the paradigm for the rest of the world.

> *Speaking about the overthrow of apartheid*
> *and the transition that followed.*

On the New South Africa

You keep trying to remind people that it's
a rainbow because the colours ... remain
distinct but related. They hold together in
their difference. And their differences are
important ... you ought to be glorying in them.
It speaks of something that has to be evolving,
it's not static. It is idealistic in a way. You're
saying we want to reach a point where we
celebrate what we are, and yet know we can't be
who we are unless you can be who you are.

The road ahead may be long and hazardous but
at long last it seems that what so many have
prayed and fasted for, sacrificed and died for,
were imprisoned, banned and went into exile
for ... seems more attainable than ever.

A widow cups the president's face in the palms
of her hands and looks into his eyes after he has
spoken movingly in Afrikaans at the funeral of
her wonderful husband – Beyers Naudé – the
picture of the two of them speaks so eloquently
of the kind of nation we want to be.

Today in our beautiful land it is the Constitution that has the last word and our highest court, the Constitutional Court, can strike down any piece of legislation which it declares unconstitutional – we could not have parliament pass a law to bring back the death penalty for instance.

> *Tutu singles out a significant achievement of post-apartheid South Africa, during his 2008 Dullah Omar Memorial Lecture at the University of the Western Cape.*

There is a lot of hurt – the Truth and Reconciliation Commission did a little bit but there are umpteen people who have been hurt in one way or another.

Honouring ubuntu is clearly not a mechanical, automatic and inevitable process, and we in South Africa have been blessed with some quite remarkable people of all races, not just black South Africans.

We were involved in the struggle because we believed we would evolve a new kind of society. A caring, a compassionate society. At the moment many, too many, of our people live in gruelling, demeaning, dehumanising poverty. We are sitting on a powder keg.

The powder keg allusion echoes a phrase he used in a letter to then president B. J. Vorster in 1976 describing conditions in South Africa.

We will succeed because God wants us to succeed for the sake of God's world. For we are so utterly improbably a beacon of hope for the rest of the world.

We have a wonderful country with wonderful people. We have the potential to become a vibrant land responsive to the needs of its peoples, caring and compassionate, in which each know they matter. A country that belongs to all who live in it, in which the people shall indeed rule. Let us take back our country.

Our friends who helped us become free are dismayed by our extraordinary postures internationally, represented by our very odd vote with China and Russia against a non-punitive resolution in the United Nations Security Council on Burma and our policy towards Zimbabwe. It all seems such a betrayal of our ideals and our past.

Sadly we have continued a mindset that was appropriate for fighting apartheid, whose laws were immoral, and so not obliging obedience. Thus we made South Africa ungovernable. We are by and large still not what we should be now, law abiding citizens, because these are our laws made by our representatives. Very few of us obey all the traffic laws, just look at how we speed and the resulting carnage is not surprising.

My father used to say, 'Improve your argument, don't raise your voice.'

> *Tutu laments what he characterised as the unfortunate consequence of a history understandably strongly tinged with a disrespect for the law, during his 2008 Dullah Omar Memorial Lecture at the University of the Western Cape.*

An Irish millionaire every year brings out at their own cost 300 or so fellow Irish and they build 50 beautiful houses in a week costing R48 000 each. Why can't South Africans do the same?

Fantastic! That image of the Springboks carrying our president shoulder high; wasn't that just something? What makes it even more powerful is that it was spontaneous and unrehearsed. That spoke volumes about our beautiful land, our rainbow nation and its potential.

We have all left the house of apartheid's bondage. Some, an élite few, have actually crossed the Jordan into the Promised Land. Others, too many, still wallow in the wilderness of degrading, dehumanising poverty ... Much has to be done. People have clean water and electricity who never had these before, but we are sitting on a powder keg because the gap between the rich and poor is widening and some of the very rich are now black.

We are the epicentre in many ways. We have high levels of crime, levels of poverty that are unacceptable, and then the usual bangshoot of corruption and things of that sort. So they have a very full plate to deal with; one must wish them well for everybody's sake. The [ANC-led government] has to succeed.

On the South African Council of Churches

If [the apartheid government] take on the South African Council of Churches then you must know that they are taking on the Church of God and other tyrants before them have tried to destroy the church – Nero, Amin, Hitler, Bokassa, etc. ... Where are they today? They have bitten the dust ignominiously. I warn the South African government again – they are not gods, they are mere mortals. Who will end up as mere marks on the pages of history, part of its flotsam and jetsam. I am not afraid of them.

I could not possibly try to emulate my predecessor [as general secretary] and so I can only do and be what I know best, and that is to be myself. [My wife and I] have come to this job with considerable trepidation.

Speaking after his appointment as Anglican Archbishop of Cape Town in 1985.

At the risk of sounding like a cliché-ridden creature, I hope that God will be able to use us as one of his instruments for justice and reconciliation; to be like those who demonstrated their solidarity with the poor and down-trodden and, as far as possible, to be a voice for the voiceless ones.

My purpose is to demonstrate from the Scriptures and from hallowed Christian tradition and teaching that what we are as the South African Council of Churches, what we say and what we do, that all of these are determined not by politics or other ideology ... We in the SACC believe absolutely in the centrality of the spiritual; that we are not just a bunch of activist do-gooders engaged in the social gospel. We have as our example and paradigm the Son of God Himself, who spent whole nights in prayer, had retreats, and then concerned Himself to meet human need ... Every Wednesday at lunch time we have prayers for justice and reconciliation in our land.

> *Testifying before the 1982 apartheid-era commission into the organisation.*

On Spirituality

Recently I have been discovering again the tingling joy of the Gospel that I have to do nothing to gain acceptance by God. That it is his acceptance of me which enables there to be me and for there to be acts and for there to be thoughts and words by me. One ought to have a semi-Cartesian dictum: 'I am loved therefore I am.'

On the Anti-apartheid Struggle

We are involved in a moral struggle. We are involved in a struggle that will succeed. We have no doubt that we are going to be free. Because we know we are going to be free, we can afford to be disciplined and we need to underline the fact of this struggle being a non-violent struggle. Therefore I ask you, when we finish here, I ask you to disperse peacefully, quietly, in a disciplined way.

Many more will be banned. Many more will be deported or killed. Yes, it will be costly. But we shall be free. Nothing will stop us becoming free – no police bullets, dogs, tear-gas, prison, death. No, nothing will stop us because God is on our side.

I can't prescribe what you must do. You have to have the sensitivity of love not to hurt people's pride. Don't be a do-gooder. Sometimes all that is necessary is to visit a banned or detained person and show that you do not fear contamination and that you don't fear the system.

My passionate opposition to apartheid stems from my understanding of the Bible and the Christian faith. If anyone can prove that apartheid is consistent with the teachings of the Bible and Jesus Christ then I will burn my Bible and cease forthwith to be a Christian. Praise to God that no one can do that.

You do not want biblical exegesis every time you ask me a question, but I think I have to indicate to you that liberation, setting free, is a key concept of the Bible. The paradigmatic event in the Bible is the Exodus, of setting free of a rabble of slaves ... we are participating in God's glorious movement of setting people free.

Our children are being used as hostages in the power game of the government of South Africa. By controlling our children, the government hopes to control the parents. I am not just talking about black children, though they are by far the group that suffers the most. I speak also of white children who learn to hate at a very young age, who learn to salute, to march, to fear children with black skin, who are being trained in their bodies and their minds and their spirits to prepare for war.

The system knows how to turn us against ourselves.

> *Speaking about protests by anti-imperialist Black Consciousness activists, which embarrassed Tutu in his attempt to show undivided opposition to apartheid by as many as possible, during an address by Senator Edward Kennedy, at the famous Regina Mundi Cathedral in Soweto in 1985.*

I find it disgraceful that Denmark is buying South African coal and increasing a dependence on South Africa, whereas one would hope that we could get South Africa to having a weaker position in bargaining, so that we could get this change as soon as possible.

Why don't we use methods of which we will
be proud when our liberation is attained? This
undermines the struggle.

> *Tutu frantically addressing a crowd of*
> *infuriated youths intent on killing a member*
> *of their community who they alleged was*
> *a police informer – and in the ensuing*
> *confusion saved the man's life.*

[Young people] have, they believe, sat for too
long, listening night after night to the stories of
their parents' daily humiliations just because
they were black. They have decided that enough
is enough. They are people with iron in their
souls.

The outside world is hoodwinked if it thinks
that by recognising black trade unions,
government has begun to liberalise apartheid.
It has done nothing of the sort. It realised that
with the interest of multi-national corporations
in the work situation it had to do something.
Legislation will attempt to undermine the
unions and curb them. The black unions have
said they will defy any laws that intend to turn
them into toothless bulldogs, and the SACC has
said that it will want to be supportive.

When a pile of cups is tottering on the edge of the table and you warn that they will crash to the ground, in South Africa you are blamed when that happens.

We want political participation, not petty dispensation. We want a completely integrated society.

Basically I long and work for a South Africa that is more open and more just; where people count and where they will have equal access to the good things in life, with equal opportunity to live, work and learn. I long for a South Africa where there will be equal and untrammelled access to the courts of the land, where detention without trial will be a thing of the hoary past, where bannings and such arbitrary acts will no longer be even so much as mentioned, and where the rule of law will hold sway in the fullest sense.

We will be free! All of us! Black and white together! We are the rainbow people of God! We are unstoppable! Nobody can stop us on our march to victory! No one, no guns, nothing!

Nothing will stop us, for we are moving to
freedom! We are moving to freedom and nobody
can stop us! For God is on our side!

> *Closing statements to an emotional but
> extremely volatile crowd at the funeral of a
> senior ANC leader, Chris Hani, who was
> assassinated by a right wing anti-Communist
> extremist on the eve of the historic 1994
> democratic elections.*

I got involved in a liberation struggle and
ended up on the winning side, and I'm alive
to experience it. And then being invited to
preside over a process of trying to heal a nation
(the TRC) – it was an incredible privilege.
And before that to have been the person to
introduce Nelson Mandela to South Africa and
to the world as our new democratically elected
president – there's nothing you can give for
those experiences. It's been fantastic.

We are free today very largely because of the
wonderful support that we received from the
international community ... You made a telling
contribution.

On Allowing Suffering

It is to spit in the face of God.

On Theology

It is salutary to be reminded yet again that
all theology is provisional, contextual and
particular.

On Tibet

For God's sake, for the sake of our children, for
the sake of their children, for the sake of the
beautiful people of Tibet – don't go. Tell your
counterparts in Beijing you wanted to come but
looked at your schedule and realised you have
something else to do.

> *Calling on world leaders to boycott the Beijing
> Olympic Games, as a moderated response to
> bring attention to the Chinese government's
> treatment of the Tibetans.*

On Tolerance

Despite the obvious fact that, for instance,
Christians do not have a monopoly on truth

or virtue and that adherents of other faiths do happen inconveniently to be people of unarguable goodness, probity and holiness, to have access to truth, many Christians hold to the view that non-Christian faiths are devoid of all truth and even that they are paganism of the worst kind ... is God really any less honoured that the Dalai Lama happens to be a transparently holy and serene Buddhist? ... In our opposition to apartheid our greatest allies were often not Christians but people of other faiths.

On the Truth and Reconciliation Concept

Our country's negotiators opted for a 'third way' that avoided the two extremes of the Nuremberg trials and blanket amnesty (or national amnesia). This third way was the granting of amnesty to individuals in exchange for full disclosure relating to the crime for which amnesty was being sought.

Ubuntu means that in a real sense even the supporters of apartheid were victims of the vicious system which they implemented and which they supported so enthusiastically ... in the process of dehumanising another, in inflicting untold harm and suffering, the perpetrator was inexorably being dehumanised as well.

This kind of justice seeks to rehabilitate both the victim and the perpetrator, who should be given the opportunity to be reintegrated into the community he or she has injured by his or her offence.

Truth: the first part of reconciliation

Those who have wronged must be ready to say, 'We have hurt you by this injustice, by uprooting you from your homes ... by giving your children an inferior education ... we are sorry; forgive us.'

Forgiveness by the victims: the second part of reconciliation

Gospel imperative.

Reparations: the third part of the reconciliation process

If I am truly repentant, I will demonstrate this genuine repentance by returning your pen.

Saying sorry is not an easy thing to do. We all often hedge our apologies. We should be magnanimous and accept it as a magnanimous act.

Here the central concern is not retribution or punishment but, in the spirit of ubuntu, the healing of breaches, the redressing of imbalances, the restoration of broken relationships.

Let us go ... the Christian way, the way that says, yes there is risk in offering people forgiveness, you don't know how they are going to turn out. But that's not ... our business, that's God's business, with that particular individual.

Often there have been those who have wanted to provide a spurious kind of reconciliation ... a papering over of the cracks instead of dealing with the situation as it demands, seriously facing up to the unpleasantness of it all ... Glorious Gospel words have fallen into disrepute and been horribly devalued so that many have come to think that 'reconciliation' meant making peace with evil, immorality, injustice, oppression and viciousness ... Quite rightly they have rejected such a travesty of the genuine article ... How could anyone really think that true conciliation could avoid a proper confrontation?

We are honoured that in these trying times the president saw fit to salute the contribution South Africans have made to deepen the world's understanding of peace, justice and reconciliation.

> *On receiving the 2009 US Presidential Medal of Freedom.*

On the South African Truth and Reconciliation Commission

This process is not about pillorying. It's actually about getting to the truth, so we can heal.

If we are to experience genuine reconciliation, then it will have to be on the basis of truth, however shattering ... In the TRC we came to realise the importance of people being able to tell their stories, for their identity was linked so inseparably with their stories.

The act, the law, that brought [the TRC] into existence, did put down as one of the things that we were to do, as part of our mandate, the granting of amnesty, and then, also, the recommendations with regard to reparations.

One of our recommendations is to say to the various sectors of our community, the business sector, the health sector, the legal profession – all of these who, in one way or another, benefited from the apartheid dispensation – you have a particular role to play in the new society, the new South Africa.

On Unilateralism

The black community can be dealt with effectively only through its recognised leaders. Anything else the government attempts will be like fiddling while the fires of revolution burn in our country.

When does compassion, when does morality, when does caring come in? I just hope one day that people will realise that peace is a far better path to follow. Many, many of us are deeply saddened to see a great country such as the United States aided and abetted extraordinarily by Britain. I have a great deal of time for your prime minister but I'm shocked to see a powerful country use its power frequently, unilaterally. The United States says: 'You do this to the world. If you don't do it, we will do it' – that's sad.

> *In 2003 Tutu revealed his feelings about the planned invasion of Iraq on The Jonathan Dimbleby Programme.*

On the USA

I didn't know anything about baseball, but what mattered was that a black man [Jackie Robinson] had made it against huge odds. I was sold on America from then on.

[President Reagan's dismissal of the call for sanctions against South Africa] did not make me anti-American. We appealed over the head

of the president to the American people, and
soon afterward Congress passed anti-apartheid
legislation.

There are many, many good things about you.
To have a woman party presidential candidate
[Hillary Clinton] who is a worthy candidate
in her own right. And Obama, that he should
seem to have energised so many young people
to be involved in politics in a way that hasn't
happened before. So, I mean, it is a tremendous,
tremendous feather in the cap of your country.

I speak as one who has not just admiration but
a big love for this country.

On Violence

A devilish deed – low and despicable.
> *Tutu's reaction to an attack on white South
> Africans in a Cape Town church at the height
> of violent reprisals between radical elements,
> during the negotiated settlement.*

The reprisal against the suicide bomber does not
bring peace. There is a suicide bomber, a reprisal

and then a counter-reprisal. And it just goes on and on.

On the War on Terror

You can never win a war against terror as long as there are conditions in the world that make people desperate – poverty, disease, ignorance, et cetera. I think people are beginning to realise that you can't have pockets of prosperity in one part of the world and huge deserts of poverty and deprivation and think that you can have a stable and secure world.

[President Bush should have responded to the 9/11 attacks] not as an act of war, but as an egregious crime. The perpetrators should have been apprehended and tried before an international criminal court. If that had happened, the whole world would have cooperated.

According to the rules of war, there has to be a nation, so Iraq was recruited ... The emergence of an enemy galvanised US patriotism.

Are you able to restore to those people the time

when their freedom was denied them? If you
have evidence, for goodness' sake produce it
in a court of law. People with power have an
incredible capacity for wanting to be able to
retain that power and don't like scrutiny.

> *Speaking after the release of a United
> Nations report calling for the closure of
> Guantanamo Bay prison camp.*

On His Weaknesses

There are not too many who enjoy being
castigated as ogres, as someone others love to
hate. I think that most of us would prefer to
be popular than unpopular. I know for myself
that it has tended to be a weakness – a tendency
to enjoy the limelight, a weakness that would
make you soften things that are hard but that
you need to say. Many people would be surprised
that, in fact, I'm quite shy. I know it doesn't
look like it.

On His Wife

Wonderful, so supportive. There must have been
many moments when she must have wondered
what she'd done!

On White South Africans

I don't think many of you really believe that
you are people of infinite worth. Because you
don't realise this you tend to behave like bullies.
Bullies throw their weight about to make
their mark. Whites amass material wealth to
prove their worth. But you have infinite worth
because God has created you in his image. If
you would only believe it of yourselves, you
would believe it of others.

I understand why white people have the kind
of perceptions they have, which are totally
different from the perceptions of blacks. If my
wife and I had lived in the northern suburbs
of Johannesburg always, what would we know
about the state of emergency?

What do you really know about Communism or
Marxism? You are brainwashed by that awful
public service SABC and that voice on Current
Affairs which constantly misleads you as it does
its propaganda work for the Nationalist Party.
And you just sit around and do nothing about it.

*Speaking to students at the University of the
Witwatersrand in 1980.*

White South Africans under apartheid made the big mistake of confusing 'legal' with 'morally right', and thus would get very hot under the collar when I and others said unjust laws did not oblige obedience.

Throw off your lethargy and the apathy of affluence. Work for a better South Africa for yourselves and for your children. Uproot all evil and oppression and injustice of which blacks are victims and you whites are beneficiaries, so that you won't reap the whirlwind. Join the winning side. Oppression, injustice, exploitation – all these have lost, for God is on our side – on the side of justice, of peace, of reconciliation, of laughter and joy, of sharing and compassion and goodness and righteousness.

There is no such thing as separate freedom – freedom is indivisible. At the present time we see our white fellow South Africans investing much of their resources to protect their so-called freedom and privileges … These resources could be employed in more creative ways to improve the quality of life of the entire community.

Be nice to the whites, they need you to
rediscover their humanity.

White South Africans are not demons. White
South Africans are ordinary human beings.
Most of them are very scared human beings,
and I ask this audience, 'Wouldn't you be scared
if you were outnumbered five to one?'

In many ways it was whites who needed to
hear the message about self-reassurance and
self-acceptance, that oppression dehumanised
the oppressor as much as, if not more than, the
oppressed.

Most of the victims [of the HIV/Aids
pandemic] are blacks and you would have
thought given where we come from that whites
would say, 'Good riddance to bad rubbish.'
Quite the contrary, many of the most dedicated,
most committed workers in the anti-HIV/Aids
campaign are whites.

> *Tutu characteristically points out the*
> *good amidst the bad; here on the occasion*
> *of the second Nelson Mandela Annual*
> *Lecture, organised by the Nelson Mandela*
> *Foundation.*

On Women

The fulfillment of God's dream for human
beings happens in the new dispensation when
we are incorporated in Christ where 'there is
neither Jew nor Gentile, slave nor free, male nor
female, but we are all one in Christ'. Thus, it is
not trying to be in vogue – to be climbing the
latest bandwagon – to be concerned about the
place for women in society and in the church.
There can be no true liberation that ignores
the question raised by the movement for the
liberation of women.

I believe that males and females have distinctive
gifts, and both sets of gifts are indispensable for
truly human existence. I am sure the church has
lost something valuable in denying ordination to
women for so long ... Somehow men have been
less human for this loss.

I would like to refer to one aspect – a
tremendous quality that women have – which
relates to the quality in God. It is the faith
women have in people. Take a child who is a
cause of much frustration and disillusion in
others. The mother of that child can see the

beauty and goodness hidden deep down, and women are much more patient than men in trying to bring that goodness to the surface. They have the capacity, more than men, to cherish that good and bring it to fruition. Women, we need you to give us back our faith in humanity.

[When I visited Rwanda after the 1994 genocide I witnessed] some women beginning to build a settlement, which they named the Nelson Mandela Village. It was to be home for some of the many widows and orphans created by the genocide. I spoke to the leaders of the women's movement that had conceived this project. They said, 'We must mourn and weep for the dead, but life must also go on, we can't go on weeping.' How wonderfully impressive, how indomitable. [Where I had been in Ntarama before witnessing the results of the brutality], we might say, there was Calvary, death and crucifixion. Here in the Nelson Mandela Village was resurrection, new life, new beginning, new hope. Again it was noteworthy how women have this remarkable resilience and an instinct for nurturing life.

On His Work

It's not histrionics, but I have to get myself into that particular moment. And my inclination would be to keep quiet and not muddy the waters. I depend upon and am sustained so utterly by so many people, and I am fortunate enough to have been trained by a religious community for the priesthood and saw how crucial for them the spiritual life was – so one has sought to emulate them. Without that resource, I would have been done for long ago.

As a Christian you are a prisoner of hope not because you are able to gaze into a crystal ball, but because of the death and resurrection of Jesus. Nothing could have been more hopeless than Jesus hanging on the Cross on Good Friday. Easter happened and Christians forever have to know that there is no way in which injustice is going to prevail over justice, or evil prevail over goodness, or death over life – despite all appearances to the contrary.

I am Christian because I have been incorporated into a body that means that my relationship with God also has social, political and economic dimensions. My love of God must be

authenticated and expressed through my love
of neighbour ... I am really saying to people
that if you don't want to be involved politically,
economically and socially, then don't worship
the Christian God ... I would find it very
difficult, if not impossible to worship a God who
did not care that people did not have rent, or
were unemployed or were oppressed.

On the Political Crisis in Zimbabwe

We Africans should hang our heads in shame.
How can what is happening in Zimbabwe
elicit hardly a word of concern let alone
condemnation from us leaders of Africa? After
the horrible things done to hapless people in
Harare, has come the recent crackdown on
members of the opposition ... what more has to
happen before we who are leaders, religious and
political, of our mother Africa are moved to cry
out 'Enough is enough'?

What an awful blot on our copy book. Do we
really care about human rights, do we care that
people of flesh and blood, fellow Africans, are
being treated like rubbish, almost worse than
they were ever treated by rabid racists?

Sources

Articles from the following mass media and other sources: *Financial Mail*, Anglican Communion News Services, Sapa, *New Internationalist*, *City Press*, *The East African*, *UK Quaker Journal*, *The Observer*, *The Mail and Guardian*, Minnesota Public Radio, *Frontline*, BBC, Politicsweb, PRNewswire, *New York Times*, *The Guardian*, *Seattle Post*, SA History, SAInfo, *Harvard University Gazette*, Gastrow, S. (1985) *Who's Who in South African Politics*, Johannesburg: Ravan; Hayes, S. (ed) (2000) *Who's Who of Southern Africa 2001*, Johannesburg: Jonathan Ball; Shirley du Boulay (1988) *Tutu: Voice of the Voiceless*, London: Hodder and Stoughton Ltd; Naomi Tutu (1989) *The Words of Desmond Tutu*, New York: New Market Press; John Allen (2006) *Rabble-Rouser for Peace: The Authorised Biography of Desmond Tutu*, Rider Books; Tutu, D. (2005) *God Has a Dream*; Tutu, D; Tutu, D. (2009) *God's Dream*; Sparks, A (1995) *Tomorrow is Another Country*, Heineman: London; Crawford-Brown, T. (2007), *Eye on the Money*, Roggebaai: Umuzi; Gevisser, M. (2007) Thabo *Mbeki: The Dream Deferred*, Craighall: Jonathan Ball. Letter to Prime Minister B.J. Vorster, 1976; Memorial address for Steve Biko,

1977; Oration at Steve Biko's funeral, 1977; Robert Sobuke funeral address, 1978; Fifth Anniversary of the Republic? speech, *1981*, The Divine Intention: presentation to the Eloff Commission of Enquiry, 1982; Crying in the Wilderness speech, Tutu, D, 1982; Hope & Suffering: Sermons & Speeches, Tutu, D, 1983; Interview: Leadership magazine, first quarter, 1985; The Rainbow People of God,Tutu, D, 1994; Let us celebrate diversity: the tenth Desmond Tutu Peace Lecture, Tutu, D, 1994; No Future Without Forgiveness, Tutu, D, 1999; 2nd Nelson Mandela Annual Lecture Address, 2004; 'Goodness Triumphs Ultimately': Warren and Anita Manshel Lecture in American Foreign Policy, 2007; 'The State of Our Democracy': Dullah Omar Memorial Lecture, 2008; Many forewords & other contributions to books & journals.